The German Shepherd Dog

Esther Verhoef

The German Shepherd Dog

REBO
PUBLISHERS

© 1998 Zuid boekprodukties
© 2006 Rebo Publishers

Text: Esther Verhoef
Photographs: Esther Verhoef
Cover design and layout: Mesika Design, Hilversum, The Netherlands
Typesetting and pre-press services: AdAm Studio, Prague, The Czech Republic
Americanization: David Price for First Edition Translations Ltd, Cambridge, UK
Proofreading: Sarah Dunham

ISBN 13: 978-90-366-1558-7
ISBN 10: 90-366-1558-5

CONTENTS

1 History 6
Herding dogs 6
Phylax 6
Max von Stephanitz 8
Selection 10

**2 Characteristics of the German
Shepherd Dog**
A true working dog 14
The German Shepherd Dog
and the family 17
Association with congeners and other ani-
mals 18
The need for exercise 19
Ability to learn 22

**3 Appearance of the German
Shepherd Dog** 24
The body 24
The head 26
The coat and the coat color 28
The gait 29

4 Your puppy
The first one you happen to find? 32
Different bloodlines 34
Male or female? 36
Imprint and socialization stage 37
What to look for 38
The choice 38
The big day 41
The first night 44

5 Raising your puppy 46
House-training 46
Socialization 48
What is allowed and what is not 50
Exercise during the growth stage 55
Other aspects of raising your puppy 56

6 Training 60
Training in practice 60
Commands 63

Fetching 69
Playing... 70
Dog sports 73

7 Care 76
Basic equipment 76
Care... 79
Vermin control 83
Vaccinations 87
The daily walk 87
Swimming 88

8 Feeding 90
Different kinds of food 90
The right food for a puppy 94
Average weights 95
Feeding an adult dog 95
Switching to other food 96
Chews... 97

9 Diseases 98
Recognizing diseases 98
Hip dysplasia 100
Panosteitis 102
Back problems 103
Uteritis.. 103
Prepuce infection 105
Allergies 105
Impaction of the anal glands 110
Diarrhea 110
Bloat (gastric torsion) 110

10 Breeding 112
Prior considerations 112
The parents 112
The service 115
The pregnancy 116
Necessities 119
Birth 120
After the birth 123

Important addresses 126

1 History

Herding dogs

The German Shepherd's original ancestors were the old German herding dogs. Their task was mainly to round up and herd sheep and cattle. In earlier times, the shepherd needed a dog he could trust implicitly, that would obey promptly and perform well in every respect. If the dog was also beautiful in appearance, that was appreciated but not considered important. Therefore, when the dogs were first bred, only the best working dogs were used. Disobedient, unhealthy, and slow dogs were not given a chance. As a result of this strict selection, the majority of the working dogs were hardworking, intelligent, obedient, brave, and tough, with great stamina.

Sheepdog from Wetterau (drawing by Friederich Specht, 1872)

Phylax

Right: the German Shepherd Dog is a strong dog that can trot and run effortlessly for a long time.

Following countries such as Great Britain, the Netherlands, and Belgium, which bred internationally recognized, nation-specific herding dogs, the Germans, too, wanted to have their own, national breed of herding dog. The many breeds of herding dog in Germany, however, made this no easy task. For instance, among others, there were white, wolf-gray, uniform black, and brown-gray dogs. Not only were the colors diverse,

but also the length and structure of the coat, and the build and setting of the ears. Uniformity, a condition required to call a group of dogs a breed, was nowhere to be seen. This was also partly because the pioneer fanciers, who founded the German Shepherd club Phylax in 1891, could not agree on the qualities the new German breed should have. A number of members devoted themselves to appearance of the breed, while others mainly supported its capabilities. In 1894, the club was dissolved because of too great a difference of opinion among the members.

Max von Stephanitz

The history of our modern German Shepherd runs parallel to that of the club "Verein für Deutsche Schäferhunde," founded in 1899. The Club was founded in the name of Captain Max von Stephanitz, a well-known dog-fancier at that time, and his friend Artur Meyer, who died at a young age. Von Stephanitz is one of the most important figures in the creation of the breed. He had fixed ideas about what the national breed of herding dog should look like and what capabilities the dogs should

Pluto, a German Shepherd Dog from around the turn of the twentieth century

have; more importantly, he knew how to get most fanciers of the breed to agree. In 1900, the stud book for German Shepherds was opened. The first dog to be registered was the stiff-haired, wolf-gray male "Horand von Grafrath," originally named "Hektor Linksrhein." This male was owned by von Stephanitz and served as a model for the new national breed. Von Stephanitz and Meyer presented the breeding traits of the German Shepherd at the first meeting of the Verein für Deutsche Schäferhunde in 1899. It is striking that, in the first descriptions of the breed, rough-haired and long-haired dogs and dogs with a plain or partly white coat were also recognized, but this was later revoked.

Hector and Gritli van Wohlen

Photograph from the club newsletter, VDH (German Shepherd Dog club of the Netherlands), 1958

Selection

In the wake of Horand, more herding dogs followed that could be used in the breeding program. Because there were so many different types, it was no simple task to arrive at a virtually uniform breed. In order to steer this process to some degree, a large-scale exhibition was held annually, where the best male could win the title "Sieger" and the best female the title "Siegerin." The winners did not only have to exhibit the required appearance, for example ears carried erect, proper shoulder height, coat, and bone structure, but also had to demonstrate their excellent capacity to work. From the beginning, these exhibitions attracted many contestants and spectators, and they are still being held today. Until 1935, the President of the S.V., von Stephanitz himself, carried out the inspections. The winning males were considered so important that they set the standard for breeding German Shepherds the following season. Some males even produced eight hundred direct descendants within one year and so left a very dominant mark on the establishment of the breed. As we now know, one dog or one bloodline should not be allowed to have too much influence, because the breeding base would then be too small. This happened with respect to the German Shepherd. Besides producing beautiful dogs approaching the ideal, the excessive bloodline breeding and even inbreeding resulted in dogs with less desirable qualities, such as a weak character, light eyes, and

a generally weak constitution. The club could not ignore this and therefore dropped the "Sieger" and "Siegerin" intermittently. For example, from 1938 to 1947 these titles were not awarded, but the S.V. selected a group of top dogs which were given the name "Auslese" and could provide a wider base. Later on, both principles were combined, so that nowadays not only Siegers can be chosen but also a group of "Auslese-dogs" can be selected.

Max von Stephanitz wanted a dog that not only had the right appearance but also the right temperament and ability to work

A nice head for a bitch

Shows have played an important role ever since the breed first originated

2 CHARACTERISTICS OF THE GERMAN SHEPHERD DOG

A true working dog

The German Shepherd is the most widely used working dog in the world. Not only is this dog a mainstay for the police, customs officials, and the military, but rescue workers and the blind know that they can rely on their excellent senses and unfailing loyalty and zest for work. German Shepherds have an above-average capacity to function as tracking, rescue, and

A German Shepherd Dog being trained as a guide dog for the blind

The German Shepherd is an attentive, reliable dog

avalanche dog, as well as guard and defense dog. These dogs also excel at dog sports. Where agility, fly ball, obedience, and training are concerned, the German Shepherd holds his ground. That is not only because of his good sense of smell and stamina, extremely high intelligence, quick response, and attentiveness, but mainly because German Shepherds are unconditionally loyal to their master and like to please him. They are relatively quick to understand how to do this. The German Shepherd is, therefore, a true working dog that wants to live for, but especially with, his master. That is why this breed is suitable for many people, although certainly not for everyone.

German Shepherds and the family

German Shepherds like to be a part of the family. This does not mean that the dog has to stay inside the house. German Shepherds can be kept very well in an outside kennel in a frost-free place, though this is not ideal if the dog has to stay there most of the day. Most German Shepherds adore their masters. If such a dog is forced to live isolated from the family, it will experience this as severe punishment. German Shepherds often develop a definite preference for one family member, but they are also fine company for other family members and will obey them as well. A German Shepherd will take on the role of guardian of the smallest family members and even gets as upset as you if something happens to them—and maybe even more. This tendency shown by most German Shepherds to be protective toward children is very touching, but also has its drawbacks. It also means that the dog will intervene when he thinks "his" child is threatened. So always keep an eye on him when your children are playing with other children. The urge to protect and guard is in every German Shepherd's blood. You really do not have to stimulate these qualities. In case of danger he will make himself heard, and if worst comes to worst he will stand right by you. It is also in their nature to follow everything that happens. Some take this so far that they follow their masters all around the house, which is not appreciated by everyone.

German Shepherds and children can be very close friends

Association with congeners and other animals

You cannot expect your dog to spend the whole day without companionship

Although not a hunting dog, the German Shepherd does possess a certain amount of hunting instinct, for as a breed it is interested in all living things. It is up to you to steer his attitude toward other animals in the right direction. In practice, this means that your dog has to be properly socialized at an early stage. If you have taught your dog not to go after cats, sheep, and cattle, but also that he should not be afraid of them, you should not expect any problems in his association with other animals. Most of them will generally behave well

with other German Shepherds and they seldom attack other dogs. An exception may be a very dominant or untrained German Shepherd, or a dog that sees his master giving more attention to another dog. Then envy might surface, because dogs of this breed like to be your number one. Your dog expects just as much unconditional loyalty from you as he gives to you.

The need for exercise

German Shepherds have a more than average need for exercise. Assume that you will have to walk the dog for at least an hour a day. There are numerous possibilities for this. German

German Shepherds
can get along well
with congeners,
but their master
comes first

Shepherds are trotters; this is their natural gait and it suits them very well. A well-built German Shepherd in good shape can trot next to your bicycle for miles without sign of fatigue. Of course, you will have to build this up slowly. An athlete who has not done any exercise for a year would be unable suddenly to run a marathon , and this is also true of your dog. Swimming is another good way to meet his need for activity, especially on hot days.

Most German Shepherds like to fetch, in the water as well as on land. In addition to the usual daily walks, you can let your dog run through the woods and fields unleashed. It is not in the German Shepherd's nature to run far away from you and, if you have good contact with your dog, he will not.

*Right: German
Shepherds love to
swim*

German Shepherd Dogs need a lot of activity

Ability to learn

Most German Shepherds have a natural talent for several disciplines in dog sports, but they will not do the work themselves. Just like all other dogs, a German Shepherd needs thorough training to develop his inherent qualities to the full. The high degree of intelligence, attentiveness, and the will to work for the master, make the training and instruction of a German Shepherd pleasant. So you do not have to be an accomplished dog trainer in order to teach your dog new things. He knows how to interpret your intentions in the right manner quickly and, more to the point, he likes to do it. An important condition, however, is that the mutual bond is good and that the dog has confidence in you. For that, you always have to be honest and clear with your dog and you should never tease him. A German Shepherd that is happy with his master and has been well trained and properly brought up has a blind trust in his judgment and obeys unconditionally and promptly.

The German Shepherd is an intelligent dog that does its very best to understand what you want from him

*Their intelligence
and enthusiasm for
work makes it
a real pleasure to
train these dogs*

3 THE APPEARANCE OF THE GERMAN SHEPHERD DOG

The body

The German Shepherd is a muscular, medium-sized dog that is a bit longer than it is tall. The ideal shoulder height is 24.5 inches (62.5 centimeters) for males and 22.5 inches (57.5 centimeters) for females. The length of the legs comprises about 55 percent of the shoulder height and the chest depth about 45 percent. The chest is deep but not too wide, and the brisket (the part of the chest in front of the forelegs) has to be clearly visible from the side. The chest reaches fairly far backward, so that the wide, strong, and well-muscled loins are short in proportion. The belly is slightly raised. The back, including the loins, is straight and strong, and not too long between the withers and the croup. The withers have to be sufficiently high and flow into the line of the back without interruption. The croup is long and slightly oblique (about 23 degrees). The shoulder blades are long and

The ears should be pointed

The proper angulation is very important for this breed

oblique and as well-connected as the elbows. The feet are rounded, short, well-closed, and arched, with short, firm, and dark-colored nails. The German Shepherd has a strong and well-developed, dry (having a tight skin without folds or dewlaps) neck. The neck is carried at a 45-degree angle in relation to a horizontal line. The tail is dense and heavily haired and extends at least to the hock joint, but never further than the middle of the hock bone. The tail may never rise above the body and should be carried straight or in a curve above the top line.

Bitches are somewhat smaller and slimmer than male dogs

The head

The size of the head when dry should be proportionate to the body, and with males it is a little more robust. It is moderately domed, showing only a slight forehead groove. Seen from above, the muzzle and skull should each form 50 percent of the total length of the head. The bridge of the nose and the skull are straight and seen from the side run parallel to each other. The ears are set high on the head, are pointed, and always face forward. The German Shepherd has a scissor bite and should have a full set of teeth: 20 in the upper jaw and 22 in the lower jaw. The lips close well and are tight and dry. The eyes are almond-shaped, as dark-colored as possible, and may not protrude. The expression is lively, intelligent, and self-confident.

White is not a recognized color

Wolf-gray

Coat and coat colors

German Shepherds have three different sorts of coat. The stock coat is the most popular variety. The long stock coat has longer hair than the stock coat. The coat is not as dense and is not always straight. This variety is less desirable, but in some countries may be used in breeding programs if its undercoat is thick enough. The long, open-coated German Shepherd has considerably longer hair and hardly any undercoat. Since the long, open-coated German Shepherd is less protected against the weather, it is an undesirable variety. The coat comes in many colors, ranging from uniform black to black with markings, iron-gray or ashen, or with regular brown, gold to light gray markings and a black or cloudy saddle. Small white markings on the chest and the inside of the legs are allowed but undesirable. The nose area should always be black.

The gait

A correct gait is very important for the German Shepherd. He is a trotter, and this gait allows him to cover long distances without getting tired. The stride should be long and flowing and, in the ideal case, the hind legs should reach as far or further than the forelegs.

The following page: *Long open coats do not meet the standard*

There are not many uniform black German Shepherds

4 YOUR PUPPY

The first one you happen to find?

When you want to take a German Shepherd into your family, the temptation is great to buy the first puppy at the first address you happen to find. Although this could be a good address, it still is not wise to make a hasty choice. Because of the great popularity of the breed, many people breed German Shepherds, and not all breeders are reliable. You want to be proud of your dog. You expect that he will be beautiful to look at, but mainly that he has a stable and trustworthy character and is also healthy. However, if you should buy your dog at a dog dealer's or from a breeder who takes his responsibilities

Character and ability to work are partly inherited

Your German Shepherd will be part of your family for ten years or longer

Because of their physical strength, male dogs demand more training insight from the owner

less seriously, then the risk is high that your new housemate will not live up to one or more expectations. It is obviously wiser to contact the puppy section of the German Shepherd Dog club beforehand. This club can give you addresses or phone numbers of reliable breeders who can be expected to breed good dogs.

Different bloodlines

It is good to know that there are different bloodlines within the breed of the German Shepherd, which is true of many other breeds as well. A number of breeders settle for a nice appearance, while others accent the working ability. There also are breeders who strive for both qualities and train the dogs they breed as well as showing them. Both appearance and working abilities are partly hereditary. The chance that you will find a good future working dog in a litter whose parents and earlier ancestors were bred for suitability for training is greater than when you choose a puppy from a litter whose ancestors were mainly selected for a nice appearance, and vice versa. Although one does not exclude the other, it still is good to inform yourself well beforehand.

Puppies should appear lively and healthy

Male or female?

The choice of a male or a female depends on your personal preference, but also your situation. Males of this breed are clearly larger, stronger, and more imposing than the females, and so a lot of people find them nicer to look at. But they may also be more assertive, especially during adolescence, and because of their physical strength they demand more training insight and physical strength from their owner and housemates. Bitches are generally more affectionate toward their housemates and are more gentle in nature, while their smaller size makes them easier to handle. Some people find estrus so problematic, they choose a male because of it. You should know, however, that the veterinarian can solve this "problem" temporarily as well as permanently. Consider that bitches are only receptive to the advances of the male twice a year, while males are available to bitches throughout the year. Through their excellent sense of smell, they can also be overexcited for days if there is a bitch in heat somewhere in the neighborhood, which is often the case more than twice a year in heavily pop-

In contrast to male dogs, bitches urinate only when necessary.

ulated areas. Also, the way of urinating differs between the sexes. Bitches usually urinate only when necessary, while males like to lift their leg more often during their daily walks to mark their territory. If you have a neatly laid out garden, you will have to consider that the garden is very attractive for males.

Imprinting and socialization stage

Character traits are not only determined by heredity; other factors also have influence. Important stages in a dog's life are the imprinting stage, from the third to about the seventh week of life, and the following socialization stage, which ends when the puppy is about 12 to 14 weeks old. During these stages, the attitude of the dog toward the world around him is established. It is important that in those periods the dogs have been in contact with different stimuli, meaning different adults and children, congeners, and other animals. They also have to get used to the daily way of life in the house and on the street. Puppies that have been raised in a remote kennel during the imprinting stage and have only been in contact with their mother, litter-mates, and the same caretaker, are more likely to have character defects. With a lot of patience, understanding, and proper guidance, these defects can be reduced somewhat, but the dog will seldom exhibit totally adjusted behavior. It goes without saying that you should only buy a puppy from a breeder who imprints and socializes his puppies properly. This does not necessarily mean that the litter is actually raised in the living room, but it does mean that the dogs have been inside the house regularly and that they have been in contact with other animals, people, and children.

Puppies are tattooed at about seven weeks of age. No dog has the same number.

First the ears are thoroughly disinfected

The tattooed number is applied to the ear with a special tool

The tattoo is applied with long-lasting dye, so that it can still be read years later

What to look for

When you look at a litter, you should pay attention to several important aspects. The surroundings of the pups must, of course, be hygienic. Observe the bitch well. You are a stranger to her and she feels responsible for her pups, so she is allowed to be a little suspicious. However, overly aggressive and frightened behavior is not good. A nervous or even aggressive bitch does not set a good example for her pups and, in addition, her offspring might have inherited this behavior. Pay attention to the behavior of the pups, as well. Healthy puppies are curious, playful, cheerful, and open. If they are not sleepy, they like to come and meet you. They should absolutely not make a shy, disinterested, or even apathetic impression on you. Other warning signs are very fat bellies, runny nose and eyes, diarrhea, and a neglected, patchy-looking coat. Also watch how the breeder interacts with his dogs and how they react to him. You can tell a lot from that. Finally, ask to see the papers of the father as well as the mother dog, and study the HD results well to be sure that the breeder has done everything to prevent the pups from suffering from this partially hereditary disease. If all this is in order, you can safely make your choice.

The choice

If the puppies have not been fully immunized, it is possible that the breeder will not want you to touch the dogs or come too close. You can make a fuss about this, but it is the breeder's way of showing that he thinks the health of his animals is more

important than a quick sale, and there is something to say for that. After all, the breeder does not know you or hardly knows you and cannot tell whether you have been to other addresses before where conditions were less hygienic. It is often said that you should choose the puppy that comes to you first. However, as long as they are not sleepy, all healthy, cheerful pups that are well-socialized and imprinted on people will walk up to you. The first to pluck up his courage is often the boldest of the litter and can grow to be a dominant dog in need of a master with a lot of authority and insight. If you have a hard time making a choice, then trust the judgment of the breeder. He interacts with his dogs on a daily basis and knows them best. He can also tell you which dog is best suited to your situation and wishes.

If you find it difficult to make a choice, you can ask the breeder for advice

The big day

Perhaps you will be able to take the dog home straight away, because it is old enough, but most of the time you will have to be patient for a couple of weeks. Pups are tattooed at the age of six to nine weeks and, around eight to nine weeks after birth, German Shepherd pups are old enough to go to their new homes. Be sure to have everything you need in the house beforehand. A firm basket or room kennel, eating and drinking bowls, a suitable toy, the food the puppy is used to, a leash, and a collar are essential. Ask the breeder for a rag with the scent of the litter. At home you can put this rag in the basket or room kennel, so the pup will sooner feel comfortable with you. By the time you go to pick up your pup, the whole litter will already be tattooed, but a pedigree cannot be given by the breeder because the administration of that will take some time. This will be sent to you later by the breeder or brought to your home. An immunization book including when, against what, and with what vaccine the pup has been treated, a health certificate from the veterinarian, and a feeding schedule should be given to you immediately with your pup. More and more breeders also use a contract of sale in which the rights and duties of the purchaser as well as the seller are set out.

You can best pick up your puppy by car, along with someone who can take care of the pup or drive the car. If the journey is long, then stop along the way to let the dog stretch its legs and urinate if necessary, while kept on a leash. Some pups get carsick and can vomit, but if the breeder has not fed the pup beforehand, you should not expect any problems.

Take a good look around when visiting the breeder: do all the dogs seem content and well cared for?

The first time at home

If your puppy has not been fully immunized, do not take him to places where there are lots of other dogs

Once at home, you should give the puppy the chance to urinate before you take him inside. Do this at a place you will want him to continue to use in the future. The scent will remain recognizable for the puppy and the chances are that he will get an urge at that same spot during the next few days. If the puppy does something, praise him enthusiastically and say "good boy, you did pee-pee" or any other word you want to use in the future. This is a very good way of teaching your German Shepherd Dog

to relieve himself on command, which can come in handy later on. In most cases, a pup will have had only a temporary immunization, which means that he will still be susceptible to diseases. So never walk the pup in places where a lot of other dogs come, but rather in your own garden or on a grass strip that is visited hardly or not at all by other dogs. Let the pup peacefully gain some first impressions of your house in the first few hours. Do keep an eye on him, but do not walk after him or call him. Also tell your children that they have to leave the pup alone for now, and teach them in the course of time never to tease the dog, not to call him all the time, and certainly not to pick him up. Also teach them that the pup has its own place to sleep where it may never be disturbed. Dogs that have been disturbed in their sleep and have been dragged around a lot in their early youth grow up to be neurotic adult dogs. What the pup needs most in these first enervating days in its new living environment are peace, harmony, regularity, and a warm, safe place to sleep.

The room kennel

A (portable) room kennel is an ideal sleeping place for your dog. Such a kennel gives the pup a feeling of protection and you will notice that he will go to the kennel by himself when he gets tired. Good, sturdy room kennels are not cheap, but when you

A room kennel bought while taking account of growth will last a lifetime

purchase one taking growth into account, both you and the dog will profit from it for years and you will not have to purchase a dog basket. Mentally sound dogs are always clean in their room kennel and, when inside, will not be able to do any damage to your furniture while you are out of the house. Later on, you can also use the kennel in the car. Then your German Shepherd will always have a familiar sleeping place with well-known scents nearby, however far from home you and the dog may be.

The first night

The room kennel is the right place for the puppy to spend the night. To prevent accidents, you should walk your dog as late at night as possible—at which time it should of course relieve itself—and in the morning you will be there bright and early to take it out again. If your puppy was used to relieving itself on a newspaper at the breeder's, and if the kennel is large enough, you can put one in a corner. However, it is better to make a firm box yourself out of spot-welded wire netting, into which you put the kennel with the door open. The newspaper can be put outside the kennel.

The first night can be an ordeal for you as well as the pup

It is very possible that your puppy will start howling the first night. It is all alone for the first time and misses its litter mates and its mother. It often helps to wrap the rag with the scent of the litter around a warm, metal, baby water bottle. The warmth and familiar scents will help your pup fall asleep faster.

Whining

If your puppy nevertheless starts whining or howling, ignore this completely. The howling is an "assembly signal" so that he will no longer be all alone. Since your dog has to learn that he has to be alone once in a while, it is not wise to respond to his call. If he learns that howling always gets a response, the chance is great that he will continue to do this every time he does not want to be alone. He will not limit himself to the nights, but can also show his discontent during the day by barking and howling when you are out. To prevent problems in the future, you will have to be "tough" for a while.

A young bitch

5 RAISING YOUR PUPPY

House-training

Your puppy has a keen nose and smells precisely where he relieved himself the last time

You can never start house-training your pup soon enough. Always try to prevent accidents in the house by keeping an eye on your puppy the first few weeks. Pups usually relieve themselves immediately after they wake up, and sometimes after they have eaten, drunk, or played. An interested sniffing of the ground and maybe some turning around and soft noises are a sign for you to pick up your puppy and put him outside. If you do this on the spot where he has relieved himself before, the

chances are he will do it again. Do not forget to reward him enthusiastically and use a word that you will continue to use in the future, such as "pee-pee." With this you teach your dog to relieve itself on command and that is ideal when you live in a busy neighborhood.

In spite of your attention, accidents can happen indoors, because puppies do not yet have full control over their bladders. If you catch your pup in the act, do not make a big fuss, but put him outside immediately. If you punish him now it is

Right: black German Shepherd Dog

possible that he will think he cannot relieve himself while you are watching. Under your supervision such dogs will not even dare to relieve themselves outside the house. Then they will only do it out of your sight, for example behind the couch. Of course you must clean the place of the accident with disinfectant, so the odor can no longer be recognized by your dog.

If the damage has already been done, punishment is useless. The dog does not know why you suddenly scolded him—after all he is already doing something else and this can make him confused and uncertain.

Socialization

The socialization stage of the dog lasts from seven to fourteen weeks. In this important stage of life the puppy is very receptive to all kinds of impressions, which largely determine the attitude he will assume toward the world around him when mature. If at this age he learns that he has nothing to fear from

During the socialization stage, your dog must gain many different impressions

other animals and strange people, as an adult dog he will react calmly to all sorts of impressions. The reverse is also true: if your pup is scared by a cat that attacks him in this crucial stage, or by a child that pulls his ears, then socialization problems could result with respect to cats or children. So it is very important that you let your dog become familiar with all kinds of impressions, but also that these introductions pass without calamities. If you live in a busy area, the puppy will get accustomed to traffic, people, children, and noise by himself.

Take your dog into natural settings, for instance so that he can get accustomed to cattle. Do not forget to allow your puppy to become familiar with animals and situations that are not so usual. What kind of situations those may be depends on your personal circumstances. If, for example, you do not have cats and you never make use of public transport or elevators, you could let your dog experience those things. Your German Shepherd can live to the age of twelve and, in that period, a lot of changes can occur in your family situation and living environment. A poorly socialized dog can cause problems for years, which could have been prevented by making better use of the short socialization stage.

Just like children, young dogs also have to learn what behavior is and is not socially acceptable.

Guidance during the socialization stage

You will have to guide the socialization process carefully, which means that you will have to act as the leader of the pack. If the puppy is frightened by something or if you notice any hesitation, react to this with resolution and assurance, but do not console him or pick him up. You are the boss and you decide what is frightening and what is not. You are the puppy's main example, and his attitude will depend largely on your reaction. If your puppy notices that you are acting strangely, that is a sign that the situation is threatening. Demonstrate in all situations that you are a real leader for the dog. Then he will trust your insight and adopt your casual attitude.

What is allowed and what is not

The upbringing and training, but also the total relationship between your dog and the family he is part of, will depend on the way you interact with the dog. Translated into practice this means that you will always have to be honest and clear with your dog, but above all you have to be consistent. Consistency means that you never go back on a command given earlier or are satisfied with a half-performed exercise. Nor can you allow him to do something you had forbidden before. Common mistakes are, for example, letting the dog sleep on the couch or jump up against you today, but not allowing it the next day because he has muddy paws. Nuance variations are not understood by a dog; he has to wait for your reaction to his behavior. Flexible rules are very confusing to him. Strict rules (for example, he is not allowed in the bedroom and also cannot jump up against the door) have nothing to do with drilling, but are very necessary to help your dog feel secure.

Consistency sounds like a good idea, but in practice it is not so easy to follow one line with the whole family – certainly not in a family in which everybody has an independent view on what the dog is and is not allowed to do. Therefore, everybody in the family has to agree about what is allowed and is not allowed with regard to the dog, and everyone will have to keep to this so that the dog will know where he stands.

Caught in the act

During the training, but also in everyday situations, you will have to punish your dog now and then for unwanted behavior. It is very important that he understands what he is punished for. Therefore punishing should be done at the time of the act and not when your dog is already doing something else, nor

You are your dog's main example

even when he is getting ready to do something else. The dog always associates whatever is occupying him at the moment with the negative incentive, the punishment. If you come home and find the house turned upside down, or if he has had an accident, it is no use punishing him for it. What you accomplish is that your dog will associate your coming home with punishment. If this occurs regularly, then your dog will assume a low position when you come home, which is sometimes wrongly interpreted as "guilty behavior." When dogs do this, they have been punished at the wrong moment too often. Seen from this point of view, remaining angry at the dog is completely pointless. If he went to his basket obediently after the punishment or if he comes to you to lick you under your chin (a gesture of subjection) then there is no reason to keep on complaining, but all the more reason to be friendly to him again. If you have an "enterprising" German Shepherd that manages to put you in a dilemma every day, make sure that he does not get the chance to do it in the future. When you are not home, put him in a place where he cannot misbehave, such as the utility room, the hallway, room kennel, or outside kennel. Then he will always have been a good boy when you come home. This way no damage can be done to furniture, nor to the relationship with you. Many dogs outgrow this enterprising behavior in time.

With respect to rewards also, you should always give them at the moment your dog does something you can approve of, and not afterward.

Teaching proper behavior while your dog is still uninhibited is easier than trying to cure bad habits

*Black German
Shepherd puppy*

Clarity in punishing or rewarding

Another important issue is that your punishment or reward should be understood by the dog as being such. A barely noticeable stroke and a mumbled "good boy" have as little effect as continuing to say "bad boy" when the dog is not paying attention. "He does not listen," many people then say, but in most cases the owner is not being clear enough and sometimes also not very consistent. You reward with a kind voice: "Good boy!" and give the dog a well-meant stroke or pat on the shoulder. His whole attitude should radiate happiness when he receives his reward. Only then, and no sooner, has he understood you and will he repeat the rewarded behavior.

You should punish with the deepest and loudest voice possible, "Bad boy!" if necessary accompanied by one short, firm pull on the choke chain. If your dog barely reacts, then you either have found a very dominant dog, or your correction is not clear enough—a combination of both is also possible. The choke chain is often used too much and in the wrong way. The dog gets vague "corrections" all the time and in due time gets used to it. He finds the corrections annoying and awkward, but they do not stop him from continuing his activities. Try to prevent this from happening with your dog. A correction should always be followed by a well-meant: "Good boy!" if he does not do it again. The choke chain should never be used on puppies, but only when the dog is older and stronger.

Exercise during the growth stage

Your German Shepherd is one of the larger breeds and grows fast. This demands a lot from the weight-bearing joints, tendons, and muscles. During growth, defects can occur if the dog tires himself too much, has an accident (e.g. slips on a polished floor), or has to walk up and down a lot of stairs or jump. Less obvious is the fact that playing with other dogs, although this is important to a certain extent for the socialization process, can lead to damaged tendons, muscles, and joints. Puppies are inexhaustible and often play until they literally drop. Besides the danger of future bone problems, there is another disadvantage connected to playing with other dogs. A dog that is used to playing with other dogs when he is walked, is immediately fixated on other dogs when he comes outside. His interest in you diminishes automatically, which makes him less obedient outdoors. Nevertheless, with a view to the socialization

Dogs caught up in playing make the strangest movements, which can be very bad for their developing systems

Swimming is an ideal form of physical exercise

process, it is not good to forbid your dog totally to interact with other dogs.

In the first few months, walking certainly means walking short distances. Playing with other dogs is allowed, but for a short time and not with uncontrolled or large dogs. Be sure that the puppy comes home just as fit as he was on leaving the house.

You can let a young pup run next to the bicycle from about six months of age, provided that you only cycle short distances at an appropriate speed. He must absolutely not get exhausted. In connection with passing cars, you should teach your dog to walk on the sidewalk, away from the curb.

Other aspects of raising your puppy

While raising him, you teach your German Shepherd what is and what is not acceptable behavior. This is different in each family. In one family, for example, nobody minds if the dog sleeps on the couch or is present during dinner, while in others this is not permitted. However, there are rules every dog should know. Pulling on the leash, attacking other dogs, and chasing cats, of course, can never be allowed by you. Your German Shepherd should also learn that he may never, ever jump out of the car or walk out the door in front of you, before he has been commanded to do so. The command "wait" is perfectly suitable for this. Very protective German Shepherd Dogs may bark more than necessary, and you may not accept that, either. Bumping against people, doors, and cars, knocking over children, growling at the feeding bowl or bone, begging for food— these are all things you should never tolerate. Remember that teaching good behavior while the dog is still young and uninhibited is much easier than breaking unwanted behavior that has developed over the course of time. A difficult dog that obeys poorly and goes his own way was not born like that but was made so by a master who has never been consistent, and has not had enough time or insight to devote to the proper raising of a dog which may not have the easiest character. However, if you are consistent, knowing the right moment and the right way to punish and reward, then your dog will soon adjust to your rules.

Trotting beside the bicycle is an excellent way to develop good condition and muscles, but wait until your dog is fully grown before covering long distances

Your couch is undoubtedly a comfortable place to sleep but, if you have allowed this for one month, you cannot punish your dog if you do not want him to do this once in a while

The dog cart is an excellent means of transport, which the dog gets used to very quickly

6 Training

Training in practice

You have to be consistent during training. You should never go back on a command given earlier and should always end an exercise with a command that the dog has correctly followed. This also means that you should not have too great expectations. Do not demand too much from your dog all at once. Do not lose sight of the fact that following your commands properly should essentially be fun for the dog. Nothing is more upsetting to see than a dog walking dejectedly and fearfully beside his owner, preoccupied with not making any mistakes. So do your best to make the mutual contact pleasant. Do not

During training, the dog must always focus his attention on you

pressure your puppy, and make your demands in as positive a way as possible. Only train when you are in a good mood and when you have the time, otherwise you may vent your irritations, possibly unconsciously, on the dog. Training for too long a time at once also ensures that the dog will dislike it and start making mistakes. Five minutes a few times a day is more than enough in the beginning. Before you start the exercises, your puppy should be accustomed to walking on a leash and wearing a collar. Do not drag him along the street, but lure him along with delicious treats and friendly words; then your pup will get used to this in a few days. For the training, you should use a choke chain, which must be put on properly. In nature,

Right: a simple manner to control your Shepherd without having to correct him constantly is to use the Gentle Leader or Halti

This is the right way to put on a choke chain

A rough link can be folded over in this way so that you can use the choke chain as an ordinary leash

wolves correct each other by a short, fierce bite on the neck. A short pull on the choke chain is interpreted as such by the dog and is thus understood very well. Such correction will not actually be necessary with the pup, but will be used later when the dog is older and stronger. You are training a young dog and cannot make too many demands.

Commands

Coming to you on command

The very first command, which you can teach your dog from a young age, is to come to you immediately you call him. The intention is that the dog immediately stops whatever he is doing and comes straight to you without any hesitation. To teach this, you use a long leash. Let the pup sniff around a bit and then call his name, so he knows you are talking to him, and then immediately give the command "come." If you squat down, the dog will obey the command sooner. If he comes to you, reward him with an affectionate pet and a friendly word, and perhaps give him a dog biscuit. A stubborn pup may not listen immediately. Repeat the command and tug on the leash to back up your command. This makes it unpleasant for the dog

When you call the dog, he must come to you in a straight line without hesitation

to ignore your command (the tug on the leash) and pleasurable to obey (petting, friendly word).

At a later stage, you can expand this exercise by trying it without the leash. In the beginning the pup may stall, but remember: if the puppy has followed your command, no matter how long it took, he is always a "good boy." Unfortunately, many people make the mistake of punishing their dog if he eventually follows the command after stalling. The pup does not link the stalling with the punishment, but the eventual following of the command. He was punished at the moment he came to you. The result of this is that the puppy will stall even longer the next time, because there is a scolding waiting for him when he comes to you. At a certain moment, the dog will not come to you at all or will circle around you, because he is in conflict with himself. Do not make the mistake of saying "good boy" while he is still underway; only when he gets to you has he followed the command and can he be rewarded.

Always let your dog sit at the edge of the curb

A supporting gesture is sometimes necessary to make a dog understand what you mean

Nor should you try and "catch" your puppy. You will always lose this game. If your puppy does not obey, walk away in the opposite direction. Your puppy will probably follow you.

Sitting on command

You can also start training your pup fairly early to sit on command. Squat down next to your puppy and say his name first to get his attention, and immediately give the command "sit." At the same time, put pressure on the dog's hindquarters with one hand, while blocking the foreleg. If the pup sits, even just for a second, he is always a "good boy," and you should reward him enthusiastically. Do this the moment he sits, not when he stands up again. Should this become a wrestling match, keep trying until it works. The intention is that he will experience disobeying your command as disagreeable, whereas obeying your command will result in your approval, which is something positive. In the beginning, it is sufficient for the puppy to sit for a little while. Later, you can expect him to sit until you lift the command by saying "free" or "go on."

Lying down on command

For lying down on command the command "down" is used. You teach the puppy "down" when he has properly understood and obeyed the command "sit." First, you let your dog sit. Then you pull the forelegs forward with slight pressure to maneuver him into a lying position, while keeping your other hand on his hindquarters to prevent him from sliding backward. Then give the command "down." If the dog stays down, even for a second, reward him. Most pups, certainly dominant ones, will show a bit of resistance the first few times. However, if you have good contact with your puppy and he trusts you, then he will be more inclined to lie down sooner. Avoid a struggle, but do not be too lenient; try to find the golden mean. Naturally, you must also build up this command slowly. You lift the command by saying "free" or by calling his name.

Staying on command

The command "stay" can be combined with the commands "sit" and "down," but can also be given when the dog is standing. This is a very important command, because more than once it has saved the life of an obedient dog that was about to cross a busy thoroughfare. As the point of departure, you let your pup, leashed, sit or stand on the left next to you. You then give him the command "stay." If the pup continues to lie down or sit for a while, say "free." If he does not, tug briefly on the leash and repeat the command. Build this up slowly by standing a step further away from him each time, until eventually he stays in place when he is not leashed.

Your German Shepherd Dog must always listen to you, even in the company of other dogs

Make sure that the dog stays exactly in the starting position. If he creeps away or starts walking, put him back in the starting position. This is where he is supposed to stay and not an inch forward or next to it. Also with respect to staying on command, you should not make it too difficult for the dog and should prevent him from making mistakes. Let him "free" fairly quickly to prevent your German Shepherd from lifting the command by himself. At a later stage, you can demand more from the dog.

Heeling on command

The command "heel" means that the dog should walk neatly on your left side without bothering you. He should never pull on the leash, stay behind, or wander off to the side, but should always follow you with his shoulder at knee height. His speed should be adapted to yours and not the other way around. He looks up at you regularly to keep pace with you. The use of a properly attached choke chain is practically indispensable. Let

This group has learned to stay on command

the chain hang slightly and hold it with two hands at chest height. Let the dog sit down on your left, call his name to get his attention, and then give the command "heel." Then walk forward in a straight line. If your dog stays behind, lure him with friendly words or delicious treats and reward him when he walks next to you again. If he walks too far forward or to the side, tug on the leash to hold his attention and reward him forthwith if he walks beside you again, looking up at you as he should. A bag

In the beginning, your puppy may not "heel" immediately

filled with treats can serve as support if your dog responds to this. When the dog is familiar with the command, you can expand the exercise by turning right and left and stopping abruptly in between, at which point the dog must sit immediately. The principle is that the dog pays attention to you and not the other way around. If the dog accidentally steps on your toes it is not your fault—your dog should have paid more attention. He should know you so well and pay such good attention that the leash, regardless of your movement or speed, always hangs loose and never tight. You can tell very easily if your dog understands and likes the exercise, because in that case he will follow you happily, wagging his tail and looking up at you.

With this exercise as well, do not ask too much at once from your dog. Let him "free" in good time, and practice short distances. You cannot teach a pup to walk to heel but can prepare him by letting him walk next to you on a leash, while showing him treats which of course you ultimately give to him.

Fetching

Most German Shepherds like to fetch, and it is a nice way to let your dog do something for you. You can teach a pup to retrieve in a simple way. If he has something in his mouth, call him by his name and say "fetch." If he comes to you with what he had in his mouth, switch it with a piece of dry food or something else that tastes good, and then throw the object away again. If he has something in his mouth that he is not supposed to have, you react in the same way, only instead you throw something he is allowed to have. In the beginning, it is sufficient if you just stimulate the fetching. Later, you can require your dog to fetch on command. For the safety of your dog, you should always use blocks designed for the purpose instead of random twigs or branches.

Playing

Playing with your dog is not only a fun pastime, it is indispensable for building up a good bond with him. However, do not forget that

A neat fetch of a young dog

what you consider playing can be taken seriously by your dog. This is the case in the so-called "tug-of-war" game. In this, you pull on one side of a rag, toy, or thick rope and your dog pulls on the other side. For you, this is a game; for your dog, it is a trial of strength to see who is the strongest. If you keep letting your dog win, which means that he will make off triumphantly with the toy, then he will have the idea that he is stronger than you; a dominant Shepherd may then see whether he can take over the house. If you never let him win, he will soon start to dislike the game. Tug-of-war games are permitted, but make sure that you are mostly the winner.

Tracking games
Every German Shepherd is an enthusiastic tracker. Even if it goes beyond our senses, your Shepherd is actually working hard

Teach your dog to let go of things on command, otherwise it will be quite a task to get him to do this

and with much concentration when he tries to find a rag or toy hidden by you. At the various training clubs, tracking is an important part of the training process and therefore it is always advisable to stimulate your Shepherd's keen nose. In a trial, certain rules are attached to tracking and, when you plan to work with your Shepherd, it is best to contact a club early to prevent your dog from learning to track "the wrong way." If you have no such ambitions, you are free to teach your dog to track in your or his own way.

You can encourage tracking in a lot of different ways and many variations can be found. You should, of course, begin as simply as possible and put the rag or toy to be sought farther away each time, in less obvious places. The so-called "assortment trial" is great fun to do. Your dog has to find precisely the rag with your scent on it among different rags. "Search" is the right command to use for tracking.

Training for the ring

If you plan to have your German Shepherd judged at a show or club competition, you cannot start soon enough teaching your dog to put himself "in position," to have his teeth examined (also by strangers), and to trot properly next to you. If you have not had much experience with this, you can enroll yourself and your dog in a ring training course.

Dog sports

You know that your German Shepherd is a versatile dog with the capacity to score highly in several disciplines and branches of dog sports. A variety of courses and training are provided by several clubs. You can join a kennel club where you will encounter other breeds and non-purebred dogs in addition to German Shepherd Dogs, or a German Shepherd Dog club circle where only German Shepherd Dogs are trained. The activities of these clubs include training in the field of tracking, protection, and obedience.

Several clubs offer you and your dog the possibility to take courses in agility, fly ball, and obedience. You can take courses in fly ball and agility "just for fun" or in order to compete, which also applies to courses in both ordinary obedience and farther-reaching forms of obedience. Police dog training and protection training usually entail more obligations than most other training and courses. A lot of devotion, but mostly time, is demanded from you. You will have to ask yourself beforehand if you are prepared for and take pleasure in being seriously engaged in the training of your dog several times a week on the training field. Before you start one of these sports or courses, the dog should know the basic principles and in most cases you are asked to show a certificate as proof of this. The addresses of the various umbrella organizations and clubs are given at the end of this book.

Tug-of-war is a nice game but, if you always let your dog win, he will have the idea that he is stronger than you

During a trial, tracking is subject to certain rules

It is difficult to teach an old dog new tricks; if you want to show the dog later, teach him to stand properly at a young age

*Protection (appre-
hension)*

Agility

A cushion is an ideal, soft, and comfortable place to sleep

7 CARE

Basic equipment

To walk your dog, you need a well-fitting leather or nylon dog collar and a long leash. For the training, you need a choke chain, preferably one with large links as you can "lock" this type with a buckle and therefore also use it as a regular collar. You can purchase feeding and drinking bowls in all sizes and materials, but in practice the stainless steel variety is the most handy and durable. Such bowls are easy to clean and are practically indestructible. If the bowls are a size too big, the dog will not spill as much food. Because bowls that are placed on the ground can slide, there are special, handy, adjustable-height stands in which you can place them. A room kennel is always preferable to a basket but, if you still want to have a basket, choose one made of synthetic material into which you can put a horse blanket so the dog will have a soft place to lie down. A dog that has to lie on a hard surface may, for example, develop ugly calluses on the pressure spots. From that point of view, dog stretchers are also very suitable. The disadvantage of wicker baskets or beds of other soft material is that they are chewed to bits very quickly by a young dog. Once your dog has learned to do this, he will often keep the habit for the rest of his life. Only choose a soft basket when the dog has outgrown his adolescent tricks. In addition, you will need a so-called "shedding blade" for care of the coat, a dust or flea comb, and good nail clippers.

Barking on command is part of the training

Right: when you take your German Shepherd with you on vacation, you must ensure that the dog has enough room

It is better to postpone the purchase of a wicker basket until your dog has outgrown his adolescent mischief

Play ropes are available in different sizes and colors

Always make sure that a toy is strong enough, so that your dog cannot bite off and swallow pieces of it

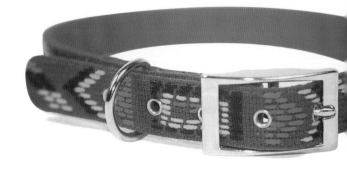

A nylon collar is stronger than an inferior quality, leather collar

Care

Care of the coat

About once a week, you should comb the coat of your German Shepherd Dog with the shedding blade. This blade works much better than other combs or brushes, because it is designed especially for double-coated dogs. If your dog sheds, you need to comb the coat every day to keep it from matting. Dogs that are kept inside all the time often shed throughout the year, which is the logical result of the constant surrounding temperature in our thermostatically-controlled, heated houses. Food quality also has an effect on shedding.

The care of the coat is not only necessary to reduce the amount of loose hairs in the house; it also strengthens the mutual bond and, during a combing, you come across fleas, ticks, and small wounds you may not otherwise have noticed.

As a general rule, washing is not necessary. If your German Shepherd Dog has got himself very dirty, you should only wash him with a special dog shampoo and make sure that he is not exposed to draft or cold with a wet or damp coat.

Pull the loose hairs out of the coat about once a week

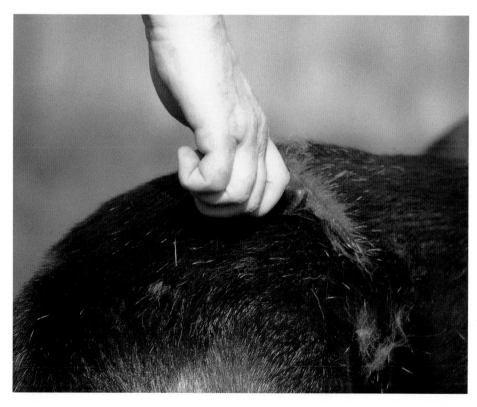

Care of nails and feet

Nails that are too long make the dog very uncomfortable. He will start to walk with spread toes, resulting in an unnatural gait. Furthermore, long nails break or split easily and that is also painful. Regularly clip the nails with good nail clippers. Try not to cut into the "quick," as this is very painful for the dog. If your dog has had overly long nails for years, then it is quite likely that the quick has grown longer; this will make painless clipping almost impossible.

Care of the nails and paws

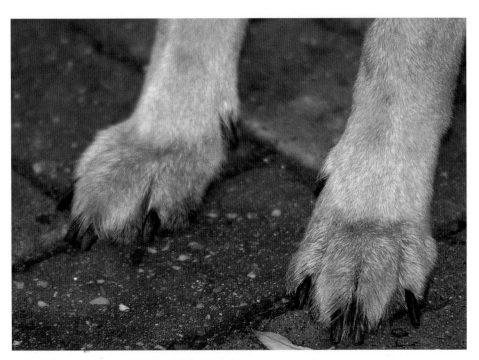

Care of the teeth

A German Shepherd pup has 28 teeth, an adult dog has 42. The pup loses his milk teeth and gets his permanent, adult teeth at the age of four to eight months at most. Check regularly that no milk teeth have got stuck and are preventing another tooth from coming through. Also check regularly whether there is tartar formation on the teeth. This will first be visible on the back teeth. A neglected set of teeth does not only cause the dog a lot of discomfort, he will also have bad breath, get toothaches, and finally abscesses will form and teeth will become loose. Light tartar can be brushed away with a toothbrush and toothpaste but, if your dog's teeth are in worse condition, take him to the veterinarian, who can remove the tartar under anesthesia. Dogs that get enough hard dry food and chewing bones have remarkably fewer problems with tartar than other dogs.

Give the dog chewing material often, because it is good for his teeth

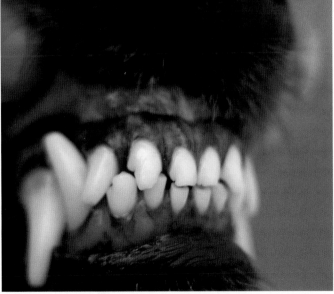

Check the teeth regularly for tartar

Care of the ears

German Shepherd puppies have slightly hanging ears that later become erect. Often one ear becomes erect first, and then the other. Ears that are drawn inward also occur in German Shepherd pups. During adolescence and the changing of teeth, erect ears can temporarily hang somewhat again, turn inward, or even fall over. This is nothing you need to be concerned about.

German Shepherd Dogs can have ear problems such as ear infections. Because these disorders are not without danger— the balance organ is located in the ear—you have to check the ears regularly and clean them when necessary. Limit the use of cotton swabs, because often the dirt is packed farther into the ear. Instead, rub the ear with an ear cleaner and remove the surface dirt with a tissue. If your Shepherd scratches his ears a lot, shakes his head, and you detect a blackish brown, grainy, and smelly discharge in the ear, your dog has ear mites. A medication to treat this can be purchased from your veterinarian.

Check the ears regularly for dirt

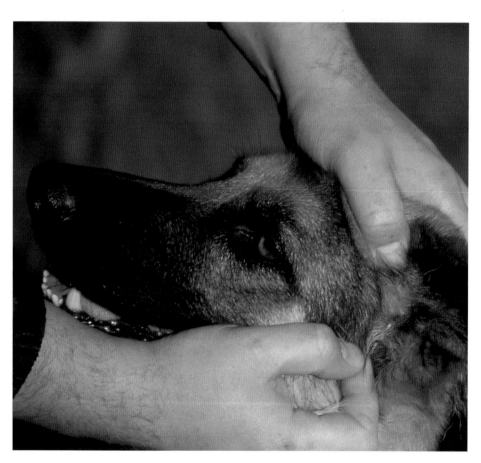

Vermin control

Fleas

Fleas are tenacious tormentors which reproduce very fast and hardly let themselves be exterminated. A dog with a flea problem scratches himself more than usual and tries to grip the fleas between his teeth. You can tell if your dog has fleas by the flea droppings. These are very visible as blackish brown grains in the coat. Unfortunately, chemical pesticides are necessary, because fleas are tough and can at the most be frightened away temporarily by all kinds of domestic remedies, but not destroyed. You can choose between shampoos, flea collars, flea drops, spray cans, and powders. One will probably work better than another and therefore you might have to try many different preparations. You can better treat pups with a flea powder that you purchase from your veterinarian.

If you know that 99 percent of the fleas in the egg, larva, or pupa stage are not located on the dog himself, but in his surroundings, it is clear that flea control does not only have to be used on the dog, but mainly on the surroundings. Because flea larvae feed on flakes of skin and other small, organic materials, you need to vacuum frequently to rob the larvae of their food supply. In addition, the surroundings have to be sprayed regularly with an anti-flea substance. Using a wet mop is of no avail—on the contrary, fleas thrive in a warm, moist environment.

Fleas are hosts for tapeworms so, if your dog has fleas, you had better have him wormed for certainty's sake.

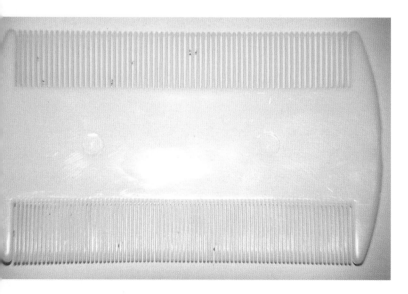

Flea comb

Removing ticks

Your dogs attracts ticks outdoors, mainly in the woods, in high grass, and in the neighborhood of bushes. These parasites drop themselves on the dog, attach themselves to the skin, and suck themselves full with the blood from the host. A tick that has sucked itself completely full is easily detectable as a gray bump in the coat of your dog. Never simply pull a tick from the coat, because the head will stick and can cause infections. Therefore, stun the tick beforehand with a piece of cotton batting drenched with alcohol, so that the jaws will loosen. Then pull it out with a twisting motion. Tick bites are not always benign, and in some cases they can transmit dangerous diseases. If you take your dog into natural areas often, make sure he is protected against tick bites by means of an anti-tick collar or some other preventive means.

Left: it can take some time before the ears are erect

Your dog gets ticks in the woods and in the vicinity of bushes

Worm control

Most pups will have already contracted worms in the litter, particularly roundworms. That is why the breeder treats his puppies for worms several times before they go to their new masters. Dogs with worms sometimes become thinner while they continue to eat normally, and in extreme cases the stomach swells up. This is sometimes difficult to see, but you will recognize small worms or tapeworm segments resembling grains of rice in your dog's stool. Worms not only damage the organs of your dog, but your children can also contract them. As a preventive measure, you should treat your dog twice a year. Always use medications that you can purchase from your veterinarian.

Have your German Shepherd Dog immunized at regular intervals

Vaccinations

Normally speaking, the puppy will have been vaccinated against diseases like hepatitis (contagious liver disease), leptospirosis, canine distemper, parainfluenza, bordetella, and parvovirus. Adult German Shepherd Dogs are usually immunized once a year. Rabies vaccination is not always compulsory in this country, but it is in some states and counties, and in many other countries. Consult your veterinarian before taking your dog on a journey. He can tell you what has to be done. In addition to the usual vaccinations, kennels often also require a vaccination against "kennel cough" (tracheobronchitis). Because kennel cough is very contagious and transmitted in places where lots of dogs are brought together, it would be wise to have your dog vaccinated as a preventive measure if you go to many dog shows or similar events. Unfortunately, the current vaccinations against kennel cough are not effective against all occurring forms.

The daily walk

German Shepherds need a lot of physical exercise, so you will have to reserve at least an hour every day for this purpose. In the course of the daily walk, you will notice that your dog likes to sniff around here and there. Dogs do this because they can learn from the urine smells about other dogs and their activity

German Shepherds love to swim and fetch; a combination of both is really fun

in the neighborhood. Scents form an essential part of your dog's environment, and therefore it would be unkind always to forbid sniffing. During training, however, he dog should pay undivided attention to you, so you should not allow it then.

Swimming

Swimming is a good form of physical exercise, but always choose a clean lake with sloping banks so the dog can easily climb onto dry land. Some dogs are rather fearful of water. If your Shepherd is such a dog, do not just throw him into the water. The chances are that he will never dare to go near water again. In the summer you and your dog can go into the water together and you can support him where necessary, so he can gradually get accustomed to it.

8 FEEDING

A dog's feeding needs are similar to those of wolves. Contrary to what many people think, wolves do not only eat the protein-rich muscle meat of their prey, but also the intestines, and they chew on bones to satisfy their need for calcium. The digestive system of wolves as well as dogs is not equipped to digest (fresh) vegetables, grains, and fruit. The vegetable remains that wolves absorb by eating the intestines of their prey, which are mainly herbivores, are already partially digested and can easily be metabolized by the digestive system of the wolf. Therefore, the vegetable ingredients in commercial dog food are artificially "pre-digested."

The dog, just like the wolf, does not only eat meat containing muscle

Different kinds of food

There are many different kinds of dog foods, which can be distinguished roughly into complete and incomplete meals. Complete meals are understood to be dog foods that contain everything your dog needs. In this case, supplementary feeding is not only unnecessary, but also disturbs the delicate balance of the various ingredients. Complete dog foods include dry food, commercially produced "dinners," com-

Right: active dogs need more food than quiet dogs

plete frozen meals based on red meat or chicken, and some canned food.

There also are incomplete dog foods that you will have to supplement yourself. Meat such as tripe or heart and several canned foods and dinners without meat are examples of these incomplete foods. If you give your dog only meat or vegetarian food, then the chances are that defects will occur in the short or longer term.

Dry kibble

Commercially produced "dinner"

Those who want to prepare dog food themselves are taking on a practically impossible task. Not only is it important for your German Shepherd to eat sufficient nutrients, but the balance between these nutrients must also be optimal. Some foods are known to prevent certain digestive enzymes from working. If, nevertheless, you still want to do this yourself, purchase a good book on the subject. In contrast to cats, dogs do not know what is good for them. They eat rotten food if given the chance and prefer products that contain a lot of salt and fat. The fact that your dog enjoys the meals you give him does not say anything about the quality of the food. Should you find it difficult to choose between all the different commercial dog foods, pick one that does not contain any artificial coloring or preservatives. More and more dogs are experiencing allergic reactions to them. An excess of protein or certain proteins can also cause

It cannot hurt to allow your German Shepherd to eat an egg now and then as a reward, but never give him raw eggs as these contain substances that hinder the action of certain essential digestive enzymes.

The digestive system of older dogs requires adjusted feeding

Diarrhea can be cured by giving the dog only rice water (water in which rice has been cooked) to drink on the first day, and the next few days only cooked rice and pieces of chicken

allergic reactions. Lamb and turkey are meats that practically every dog can tolerate without any problems.

It is a good idea to give your dog tripe, headcheese, or heart once a week. This has a positive effect on the intestinal flora. However, you should never buy this meat from the butcher, but make sure that it is specially prepared for dogs. Meat for human consumption may have come into contact with pork that could be contaminated by Aujeszky's disease (pseudorabies), which is fatal for dogs and cats.

The right food for a puppy

In most cases, you will receive a feeding list from the breeder of your puppy. It tells you how much and what you may feed your puppy and how many meals a day he needs. Because puppies have small stomachs and cannot (as yet) digest large amounts of food at once, you should feed your puppy small portions about four times a day. Dry puppy food generally has a high protein content, which is needed by young puppies up to 12 weeks for proper growth. After that, a food with a lower protein content is better.

Take care not to feed your dog too much

A (too) high quantity of protein in the feed causes the dog to grow disproportionately fast and his bones are sometimes unable to "keep pace" with this growth. The pup may suffer growing

pains or develop other problems with bones, joints, and bone sockets. If you give him fresh meat instead of dry puppy food, you also have to be careful, because meat is very rich in protein. Too much food, which makes the puppy too fat, is also detrimental to his development.

Never give the puppy or the adult dog extra calcium if you feed a complete dog food. The dog's digestive system has difficulty in excreting an excessive amount of calcium, which may then form deposits on the bones and joints with all the concomitant misery.

Average weights

The following column shows the average weight of a German Shepherd puppy in different growth stages. It does not matter if your dog weighs a little less. If he weighs more, he is then too heavy and you will have to take measures. A simple method to determine the weight of the puppy is first to stand on the scale yourself and then with the puppy in your arms. The difference is the weight of the dog.

8 weeks	11–12 lbs (5.0–5.5 kg)
9–16 weeks	an average weight increase of just over 2 lbs (1 kg) a week
20 weeks	41 lbs (18.5 kg)
24 weeks	51 lbs (23 kg)
40 weeks	64 lbs (29 kg)

Feeding an adult dog

Adult dogs are usually fed once a day, but twice is better because smaller amounts during the day can be digested better by the dog. Not all sorts and brands of food have the same energy value. The amount of food your dog needs differs according to type and brand. For example, your dog may need more canned food than a "complete" meat dinner, and dry food has a higher energy value than complete meat dinners. Moreover, not every dog has the same metabolism and the way your dog is housed (inside by the heater or outside in the kennel) and the amount of exercise also have an effect on this. So it is very possible that the nutritional needs of your dog will deviate from the guidelines on the dog food package. A German Shepherd Dog always should always look "dry." If he is in good condition, you can feel the ribs easily, but they are not immediately visible. If you have to push too far, your dog is too fat. It is generally known that, on average, overweight dogs live shorter and less healthy lives than their thinner congeners. Always try to prevent things from getting that far.

Switching to other food

In spite of the many different types and brands of dog foods, there still is no universal food which is the best for all dogs.

Stools of a different color or texture, a patchy coat, heavy shedding throughout the year, or allergic reactions can be signs that the type or brand you are giving is not in keeping with the needs of your dog. To rule out other causes, have your dog checked by a veterinarian. If he cannot find any disorders, a different food will result in improvement.

When purchasing other food, make sure that it is different in several respects from the previous food, for example the protein level, the kind of meat serving as a base, or the preservative. A different brand of the same food does not make very much sense.

If you give your dog different food from one day to the next, he will get diarrhea. The dog's digestive system will need time to adjust to the new food. For the same reason, you should not change to a different brand or type continually, but stay with the same food for several months. Improvement will not take place immediately; it can take a month or longer. You need to exercise restraint in changing foods, particularly with puppies and growing dogs, because they have not yet developed a resistance and diarrhea can cause more damage than it does in adult dogs.

This dog has the proper weight

Chews

To develop and maintain strong teeth, your German Shepherd Dog should use his teeth regularly. Bones, however, are not always safe. Bones of birds, rabbits, and pigs can splinter and seriously injure the gullet, stomach, and intestines of your German Shepherd Dog. Beef bones that have been cooked or smoked for a long time are safe and good for the teeth, provided the dog does not overdo it. This also applies to most pressed buffalo hide chews and dried piz-zle. The advantage of regularly giving such a chew, besides the beneficial effect on the dog's teeth, is that the dog can occupy himself for hours with it. However, take care that the dog does not swallow any whole pieces and that the color of his stool does not change.

Smoked beef chew

There are many types of chews

9 DISEASES

Recognizing diseases

Hopefully your dog will not get sick, but should this happen it is important to recognize that there is something wrong with your dog. In general, you can assume that you know your dog best and that you are the right person to determine whether something is wrong. Any deviations from the normal daily pattern you may observe, whether they are changes in character, changes in the eating pattern, or the degree and type of movement, can indicate an underlying problem, whether or not it is urgent. Even if you have just the slightest doubt about the health of your German Shepherd Dog, you should always contact your veterinarian. It is better to have your dog checked once too much than once too little. The following survey of various disorders and diseases is of course not complete, but contains relatively common or serious disorders.

When your dog acts differently, he may be sick

Hip dysplasia

Disorders in bone connections and joints occur relatively often in large and fast-growing breeds, and the German Shepherd Dog is no exception to this. Hip dysplasia, better known by its abbreviation, HD, is the best known of these problems. This refers to several disorders in the connection between the thighbone and the hip socket. Because bone disorders, just as character and body build, are partially hereditary, serious breeders will X-ray both parents officially before using them for breeding. Nevertheless, external influences, such as too rapid growth, the wrong food, overweight, overtaxing or wrong use of the body, or an accident (e.g. slipping on a polished floor) can have an effect on the development or aggravation of hip dysplasia.

Although people might try to ascertain from the dog's appearance whether or not the hips are in order, this disorder can never be confirmed simply by observing the dog. At the most, there can only be a suspicion. X-rays may clearly reveal the presence of HD in some dogs that run alongside the bicycle every day and are even active on the training field. There is only one way to find out if your dog has HD: ask your veterinarian to take X-rays.

There are some dogs with bad hips that cannot be seen from the dog's appearance

The manner of sitting or lying does not reveal anything about the quality of the hips

Hip dysplasia results		
The Netherlands	**Belgium**	
HD-	HD-A	HD free
HDtc	HD-B	Intermediate form
HD+-	HD-C	Slightly positive (light dysplasia)
HD+	HD-D	Positive (clear dysplasia)
HD++	HD-E	Positive in optima forma (serious dysplasia)

Signs that can indicate HD are: having trouble standing up, crying or whining when you touch the hip, and/or having trouble walking or being barely able to walk. Hip dysplasia is very painful for the dog and unfortunately there is not much that can be done about it. Operations can provide a solution, but they are usually very expensive and are only performed at a limited number of animal clinics.

Panosteitis

In some German Shepherds, panosteitis (growing pains) occurs in the growth stage. The symptoms of panosteitis include difficulty in standing up, not wanting his legs touched, and obvious pain while walking. Panosteitis is very painful. By not giving the young dog food with too high a protein level, allowing him enough rest, and making sure that he grows according to the standards indicated, panosteitis can be prevented to a great extent. If the dog is suffering from this, the veterinarian will prescribe medicines and a long period of absolute rest.

Panosteitis can largely be prevented by not providing food with too high a protein content

Back problems

Back problems occur now and then. Some examples of these are spondylosis, (neck) hernias, and "normal" wear and tear. If you notice that your dog's back is somewhat stiff, or hurts when you pat it, always see the veterinarian, who can make an informed diagnosis based on an X-ray and start the treatment.

Uteritis

There are two different forms of uteritis. One is relatively easy to recognize: the bitch drinks (a lot) more than usual, may have a temperature, and has a turbid discharge from the vulva. The other form of uteritis has the same symptoms, except for the discharge, and is often not recognized as quickly. If you suspect that your bitch has uteritis, immediately make an appointment with the veterinarian, as uteritis can remain latent for a while but eventually has fatal consequences. In a very early stage drugs may help, but in other cases the uterus will have to be removed. This infection seldom occurs with young bitches; bitches aged five years and over are most susceptible to it.

Prepuce infection

Prepuce infection occurs relatively often. It is a fairly innocent but stubborn disorder. Prepuce infection is easily recognized by

Black German Shepherd Dog

the yellowish-green, turbid discharge from the prepuce. Regular rinsing with a substance prescribed by the veterinarian will fight this disorder but, unfortunately, relief is usually temporary. As yet, there are no really efficient treatments for prepuce infection.

Allergies

Allergies occur frequently nowadays, not only in humans, but also in pets. Allergies are particularly noticeable from the skin, which becomes flaky and shows bald or red spots, and the dog usually has a bad case of itching. Because the dog keeps scratching and biting himself, he damages his skin, and often his ears as well, which can cause wounds and, later on, permanent excrescences on the skin and in the ears. Your dog can also appear to have swellings. The first symptoms generally start at the age of eight months to three years.

Allergies are one of the most difficult problems for your veterinarian to treat during his surgery hours. The cause of the allergy is not always easy to find and treat, and both the dog and the owner are driven mad by the continuous scratching, biting, and squeaking, which in severe cases can go on all night.

Dogs can be allergic, among other things, to certain kinds of carpeting, flea saliva, skin flakes, and tree and grass clumps, but

This two-year old bitch has serious problems with an allergy

there still are thousands of other substances that are less obvious and can also be the cause. The most obvious substances to which your dog can have an allergic reaction are injected by the veterinarian directly under your dog's skin in order to discover which substances the skin reacts to by swelling. Treatment can be started on the basis of these results, but is not always possible or sufficiently effective. Apart from that, some dogs scratch and bite themselves out of pure stress. Too little attention, or exercise, or, for example, a change in the family, causes so much tension in some dogs that they develop disorders resembling allergies. "Common" itch can also be the result of lice or mites in the coat and your veterinarian should of course exclude these possibilities before he does an allergy test.

Food allergies

Food allergies are a separate subject. If your dog is suffering in this way, he is allergic or sensitive to a certain amount or kind of protein or the (chemical) preservatives in his food. These disorders often start sooner than other allergies, usually even before the dog reaches the age of eight months. Dogs that suffer from food allergies or over-sensitivity itch almost continuously and often bite or scratch themselves. Sometimes small hives (urticaria) occur on bald spots that burst easily and bleed. There is a simple method to check whether your dog is suffering from such an allergy. Feed him cooked rice with cooked lamb or turkey for a period of six months. These sorts of meat are known to seldom, if ever, arouse allergic reactions. It is important that you do not feed your dog anything else in addition to this during this period. If the whole condition, but mainly the condition of the coat, improves considerably, then it is better to continue feeding your dog anti-allergenic food. Lamb or turkey with rice is not a complete food, however, and therefore you cannot keep on feeding it on its own.

Anal glands have an important function. Each dog has his own unique scent

Impaction of the anal glands

Impacted anal glands occur relatively often. The anal glands are located just above the anal opening, about half an inch inside the body. The function of these glands is to give the stools a distinctive odor that is different for every dog. Wolves also have anal glands but, because they regularly eat bones and the small, indigestible parts empty these glands in a natural way, wolves seldom suffer from impacted anal glands. Our domestic dogs have a different eating pattern, which makes the stools smooth so that the anal glands are less stimulated and become impacted. Dogs suffering from this sometimes bite

Diarrhea is not necessarily a serious matter; your dog may have eaten the wrong thing or become over-excited

themselves near the root of the tail—this can also indicate fleas—and drag their hindquarters forward along the ground with their forelegs. The veterinarian or a skillful dog trimmer can empty the anal glands in a professional manner. Some dog owners do this themselves but, if you do not have experience in this process, you should not attempt it; an unprofessional emptying of the anal glands has precisely the opposite effect.

Diarrhea

Diarrhea can have many different causes and is usually not serious. Sudden changes in the diet, drinking from puddles (also "snow munching"), eating carcasses, and also excitement can cause temporary diarrhea. In general, diarrhea will pass within a few days. A diet of rice and chicken soup, preceded by a day of fasting, is usually very helpful in getting your dog's defecation back to normal again. Give your dog enough fresh water, because diarrhea can lead to dehydration. If your dog continues to suffer from it, if the diarrhea is strongly different in color and smell, or if there are other symptoms such as weight loss or fever, do not try to treat this yourself, but contact your veterinarian immediately.

Bloat (gastric torsion)

Fortunately, bloat does not occur very often in German Shepherd Dogs. Nevertheless, it is important that you recognize the symptoms, so that you can take quick and adequate action, as bloat is fatal and proceeds so quickly that every minute counts. During bloat, the stomach turns on its axis, closing off the opening to the gullet and intestines, which causes the stomach contents to ferment. The gases in the stomach cannot escape and the stomach swells very rapidly. Because the swollen stomach pinches off the blood vessel, the dog goes into shock and dies quickly afterward. The swelling of the stomach is easy to see and to feel on the left side of the body, just behind the ribs. Dogs retch enormously and give the impression that they have to vomit, but nothing more than a little mucus is coughed up. If you suspect that your dog has bloat, every second counts. A good veterinarian knows how urgent a serious bloat is and will not be surprised if you call him for this in the middle of the night. In spite of many studies, the exact cause of bloat is still unknown. There only is a strong suspicion that it is connected with activity, or excitement after a (heavy) meal, or eating too much food at once.

10 BREEDING

Prior considerations

You have a bitch and would like to breed a litter from her. Before you start looking for a male, you will have to consider the consequences of having a litter of young dogs and what responsibilities rest on a breeder. The familiar fairy tale about the bitch needing to have had a litter once in her lifetime, because it makes her more beautiful and gentle, can be put to rest because it is nonsense. A bitch seldom becomes more beautiful; pregnancy, nursing, and caring for a large litter is a difficult event that makes heavy demands on her body. Changes in character under the influence of female hormones are just temporary and, if your German Shepherd is not gentle and reliable, she is not fit to bring a litter of puppies into this world at all.

Nor should you breed a litter to earn money from it, because that will not happen. In the period prior to the service, the service itself, the pregnancy, the birth, and during the growth of the puppies, you will have costs that are often underestimated. Expensive veterinary surgical procedures are sometimes necessary. Most breeders are already satisfied if they can cover the costs of the litter from its "profits."

Something could go wrong with the bitch, due to which you will have to raise a litter by yourself, which requires a lot of effort, time, and insight. You need to have the patience and dedication to clean up the puppies' mess several times a day, to disinfect everything, and to teach and socialize the puppies, so that they grow up to be mentally stable and social representatives of their breed.

The parents

The bitch

A good breeding bitch is without doubt a fine representative of her breed. Not only you think so, but a judge has also reacted favorably to her appearance at a club competition. Her character should be gentle, courageous, alert, and stable. Even more than the male, she has an effect on the character development of the puppies; after all, she raises the litter and serves as an example for her offspring. She is free of parasites, not too fat or too skinny, wormed, and fully immunized. Her condition as a whole can best be judged by the veterinarian, who can tell you after a thorough examination if her health will permit the

Right: a suitable breeding bitch is not only healthy and representative of her breed in appearance, but must also have a good character

pregnancy, birth, and nursing of a litter. You will, of course, have her examined for (hereditary) disorders such as heart conditions and HD. Always have official X-rays taken, because it is not possible to tell from her appearance whether her hips are good.

Your bitch is a product of her ancestors and the names on her pedigree also affect the quality of her puppies. Therefore, study her pedigree well and ascertain for yourself the health and character of the recorded animals.

The prospective father

The same rules apply to the prospective father of the litter as to the bitch. Most breeders have one or more stud dogs that have proved to be good studs with respect to appearance as well as health and character. However, it cannot be ascertained from his appearance whether the stud dog will pass on his positive characteristics to his offspring and whether these would form a good combination with the characteristics of your bitch. An experienced breeder can usually advise you on this if he has sight of your bitch's pedigree. The owner may want to see the bitch first, and you may be asked to prove her suitability through show results, HD results, and training certificates.

It is customary for service to take place on the stud owner's premises, because a male is more self-assured on his own territory, which considerably improves the chances of a successful service.

The service

You can best have your bitch serviced during the third or fourth estrus. At an earlier time she may not be mature enough physically and mentally, and older bitches having a litter for the first time are more likely to have problems during the pregnancy and birth. Bitches are in heat for three weeks, at average intervals of six months. The first signs of estrus are swelling of the vulva and slight loss of blood. In general, the bitch will only permit the service if she really is fertile, around the tenth to fourteenth day of the heat. The tenth or eleventh day is considered the ideal time for service, usually followed by a second service on the twelfth or thirteenth day of estrus. The sperm of the male stays active for 48 hours and this way of servicing guarantees the span of four days. After service, the male and bitch may remain connected to each other because the penis of the male swells up. This is called "standing connected." A bitch that is serviced for the first time can panic a little during the connection and try to pull herself loose. The animals are therefore usually kept on a leash to prevent accidents. The con-

Left: before their third or fourth estrus, bitches are still too immature to raise a litter of young

nection can take ten to forty-five minutes, but can also be absent without affecting the success of the service.

The Pregnancy

Counted from the day of the first service, the dog's pregnancy lasts 63 days. If you are curious, you can have an echogram made by the veterinarian on the twenty-eighth day. In the first four weeks, you might notice a slight change in your bitch's character. For example, she may become more relaxed, more affectionate, or moody, but not much is detectable in her appearance. From the fifth week of the pregnancy, the stomach line will change and the bitch will need more food. Because the uterus bears down on the digestive tract, the bitch cannot handle too much food at once, and you will have to feed her small portions three or four times a day. The amount of food she is accustomed to eating daily can gradually be doubled, and reduced again once the puppies have been weaned. If you walk or cycle short distances with her, the bitch will maintain her good condition, which she will need later on. However, you should avoid too much tension and exertion during the pregnancy. Do not let her jump, work intensively, or participate in shows.

Necessities

*If the
bitch is obviously
in heat, she must
receive special care*

For the imprinting and socialization of the puppies, it is best for them to be raised in the house. The living room is the ideal place, but not everybody will be enthusiastic about this. During the first two weeks, the bitch as well as the puppies only need rest and, during that period, it is better to keep them in a sep-

arate quiet place. Afterward, the puppies and the mother can be moved to a place where they have more contact with the normal daily routine. The nursery should be on the ground floor so that the bitch does not have to climb stairs. You should put a suitable whelping crate in the "puppy room." The whelping crate should be long enough to enable the bitch to lie in a stretched position, and the rims should be about 18 inches high. It should be possible to fold down the front of the whelping crate so that your bitch cannot damage her low hanging teats while getting in and out. Never put the crate directly on the floor in connection with drafts. The material you use to make the crate should be easy to disinfect. Newspapers are often used to cover the bottom, but corrugated paper is better. The puppies can get a better grip on it than on smooth newspapers.

Furthermore, you will need:
- digital thermometer
- stacks of clean towels
- a large roll of corrugated paper
- bottles and rubber teats
- a good bitch milk replacement
- bottle or jerrycan of disinfectant
- kitchen scale, notebook, and pen
- heat lamp (whelping lamp) and spare lamp

Up to the fourth week of heat, the bitch may still play and frolic; afterward, she usually becomes calmer by herself

Birth

Birth never takes place in the same way twice and complications can occur. During the last week of the pregnancy, you should take your bitch's temperature at the same time each day. The body temperature of most bitches falls by at least 1°C in the 24 hours before delivery. Some bitches become restless, start digging and scratching in their crate to make a nest, or start panting, but they will not all do this. Your bitch will have regular contractions. Within one hour of the first contraction, however, the first puppy should be born. The puppies are born in head or breach position and, as a rule, the bitch bites off the membranes and the umbilical cord, though she may also expect you to help her with this. Try to prevent the bitch from biting the umbilical cord too close to the belly of the puppy, and ascertain for yourself that the puppy can breathe. To do so, tear off the membrane at the mouth and, if necessary, remove the mucus. You should rub the puppies dry with a rough towel. Keep noting whether there are as many puppies as there are placentas. Placentas that have stayed behind can put your bitch's life in danger. Normally the bitch eats the placentas, but too many placentas cause diarrhea and therefore it is better not to let her eat all of them.

In summer it mostly is not necessary to hang a heat lamp, but in all other cases you should hang the lamp at the proper height, about eight inches higher than the shoulder height of your bitch.

A litter of puppies needs much care and attention

If the puppies strongly resemble each other, it is necessary to mark them with nail polish. If you do not do this, it is virtually impossible to follow their individual development and growth. In a separate notebook, you should record the birth weight, the gender, and the time of birth. After that, you should weigh the puppies again every day, around the same time. Any barely visible reduction or stagnation in weight that can indicate deviations or too little milk can then be noticed in time. When whelping has been completed, the bitch usually becomes more relaxed and wants to sleep. In spite of that, take her into the garden to defecate, during which time someone else can clean and disinfect the whelping crate. It would be unwise to take your bitch out on the street now because of the risk of infection. In the beginning, you should give your bitch frequent, small portions of food instead of one or two large meals, and naturally make sure that there is always a bowl of fresh water adjacent to the whelping crate.

After the birth

The first weeks after the birth

Birth usually occurs in the early evening and at night. If all has gone well, ask your veterinarian to come by the next morning to check the puppies as well as the bitch. To prevent the puppies from damaging the sensitive swollen teats of the bitch with their sharp nails, you should carefully clip the nails of their forepaws when necessary. Ascertain yourself that your bitch has enough milk for her puppies and regularly check whether her teats have become hard or changed color. Her temperature should be reasonably normal by now. If you have any doubts, contact your veterinarian. Possible dew claws on the back paws must be removed by the veterinarian within four weeks of the birth. During the first weeks of life, the puppies only drink and sleep. The bitch takes care of the puppies and cleans up their droppings as long as they are not given supplementary food or weaned.

The fourth to the tenth week

When the puppies are three to five weeks old, you can give the puppies supplementary food. Never use baby food or anything like that, but always purchase good puppy weaning food from your specialist supplier. In another week or two, you will gradually be able to accustom the puppies to eating dry puppy food. In the beginning, you should soak it in hot water so it is easy to absorb, but later on this will not be necessary. You can also give meat if it is cooked or minced. The whelping crate must be cleaned several times a day and totally disinfected at least once a day.

When the puppies are six to seven weeks old, the bitch usually pays less attention to them and may avoid them, because it is time for the puppies to be fully weaned. It is at this point that you need to have them immunized. The bitch is happy when she can go out walking with you now and again, without the puppies. The ideal age to let a puppy go to his new owner is about eight weeks.

Regularly clip the sharp points of the puppies' nails, so that they will not damage the teats of the bitch

IMPORTANT ADDRESSES

American Kennel Club
www.akc.org

German Shepherd Dog Club of America
www.gsdca.org

German Shepherd Dog Club of America–
Working Dog Association, Inc.
www.gsdca-wda.org

Orthopedic Foundation for Animals
www.offa.org

The American German Shepherd Rescue Association, Inc.
www.gsd-rescue.com

United Schutzhund Clubs of America
for the German Shepherd Dog
www.germanshepherddog.com

*A group of German
Shepherd bitches*

PHOTOGRAPHY CREDITS AND ACKNOWLEDGMENTS

The drawings were taken from Hondenrassen, Graaf van Bylandt.

The photograph on p. 10 was taken from the Verenigingsblad VDH (1958); the photographs on pp. 16, 49, 120, 121b, and 122 are courtesy of C.A. van Veenendaal. All other photographs were taken by Esther Verhoef.

The publisher and author wish to express their thanks to all those who have contributed to the creation of this publication. A special debt of gratitude is due to the Blindegeleidehondenopleiding Nederland (Dutch guide dog training), Chr. van Delft, the Van Hooff family, C. van den Nieuwenhof and family, D. Schoenmakers and Denise van Kleef, Y. Schultz, C.A. van Veenendaal and family, F. van Veldhoven and family, and D. Zevenbergen and family. The publisher and author also wish to thank the Van Riel Distripet company in Waalwijk for making their pet supplies available.

The author owes a special debt of gratitude to Mr F. van Veldhoven for his valuable advice, which has been included in this publication.